W9-BSK-059

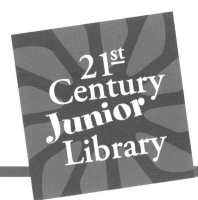

VENUS

by Ariel Kazunas

CHERRY LAKE PUBLISHING * ANN ARBOR, MICHIGAN

CHERRY
LAKE
Publishing

Published in the United States of America by Cherry Lake Publishing
Ann Arbor, Michigan
www.cherrylakepublishing.com

Content Adviser: Dr. Tobias Owen, University of Hawaii Institute for Astronomy

Photo Credits: Cover and page 4, ©Orlando Florin Rosu/Dreamstime.com; cover and page 12, ©Rolf Nussbaumer Photography/Alamy; cover and page 14, ©Philip Lange/Shutterstock, Inc.; cover and pages 10, 16, and 20, ©NASA; page 6 (left), ©Luis Stortini Sabor aka CVADRAT/Shutterstock, Inc.; page 6 (right), ©Denis Tabler/Shutterstock, Inc.; page 8, ©Matamu/Shutterstock, Inc.; page 18, ©ASSOCIATED PRESS

LIBRARY OF CONGRESS CATALOGING-IN-PUBLICATION DATA
Kazunas, Ariel.
  Venus/by Ariel Kazunas.
      p. cm.—(21st century junior library)
  Includes bibliographical references and index.
  ISBN-13: 978-1-61080-085-3 (lib. bdg.)
  ISBN-10: 1-61080-085-0 (lib. bdg.)
  1. Venus (Planet)—Juvenile literature. I. Title.
  QB621.K39 2011
  523.42—dc22   2010052612

Cherry Lake Publishing would like to acknowledge the work of
The Partnership for 21st Century Skills.
Please visit www.21stcenturyskills.org for more information.

Printed in the United States of America
Corporate Graphics Inc.
July 2011
CLFA09

CONTENTS

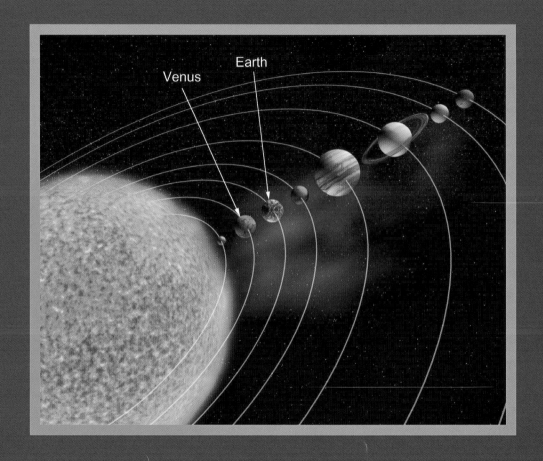

Venus is very close to both Earth and the Sun.

Earth's Twin

There are eight planets in our **solar system**. They all **orbit** the Sun.

The second planet from the Sun is called Venus. Venus is the closest planet to Earth. This makes it easy to find in the sky. We can see it when the Sun is rising or setting.

Venus and Earth are about the same size.

Venus is about the same size as Earth. It also weighs about the same amount. Even the force of its **gravity** is a lot like Earth's. Some people call it "Earth's twin."

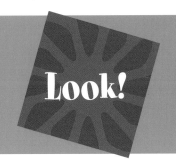

Look!

Try looking for Venus in the sky. Remember that you can see it when the Sun is rising or setting. Ask a teacher or librarian to help you find where to look.

Planets closer to the Sun have shorter orbits.

Passing Time

The time it takes for a planet to orbit the Sun one time is called a year. A year on Earth is 365 days long. A year on Venus is 225 Earth days long.

Venus years are shorter than Earth years. This is because Venus is closer to the Sun.

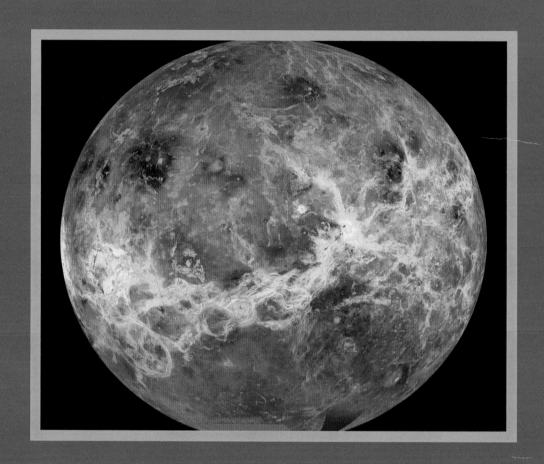

Venus has longer days than any other planet in our solar system.

All planets **rotate** on an **axis**. The time it takes for a planet to turn all the way around one time is called a day. Venus rotates slowly. This means it has very long days.

One day on Venus is as long as 243 Earth days. This means days are longer than years on Venus!

Ask Questions!

What if one year went by every day on Earth? How many years old would you be? Ask an adult if you need help with the math.

Venus sometimes shows up in the sky as a
bright dot near the Moon.

Shining Bright

Venus is easy to see if you know when and where to look. Only the Sun and the Moon shine brighter in our solar system.

There are thick layers of clouds in Venus's **atmosphere**. Sunlight bounces off the clouds. This makes Venus look as if it is glowing.

Venus was known for her great beauty.

Venus was one of the first planets to be discovered. People wrote about it thousands of years ago. They thought its bright light was pretty. So they named it after the **Roman god** of beauty.

15

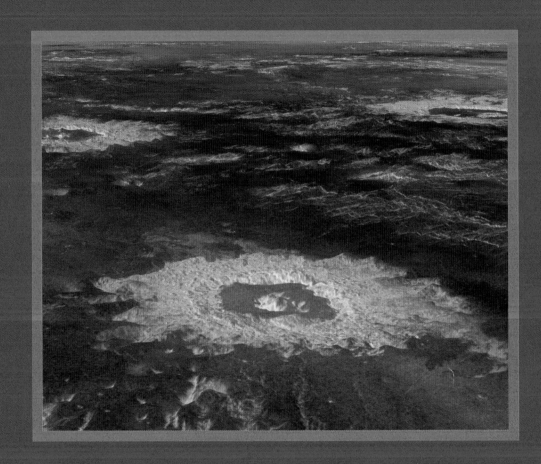

Venus's surface is too hot to support life.

Overheated

Venus is the hottest planet in our solar system. The planet's surface is about 870 degrees Fahrenheit (466 degrees Celsius) on average. The highest temperature ever recorded on Earth is only 136°F (58°C)!

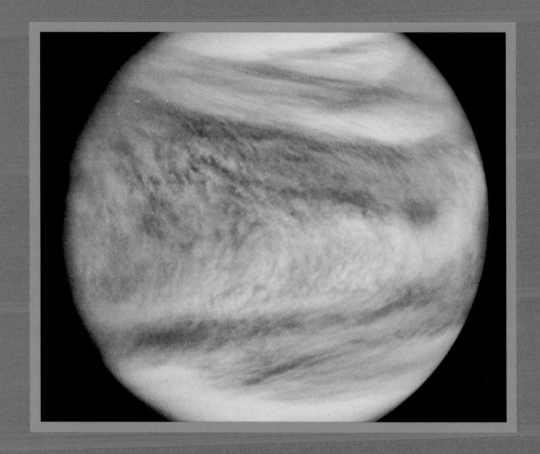

Venus' thick, cloudy atmosphere makes it very hot.

Why is Venus so hot? Remember that Venus has a very thick atmosphere. This atmosphere acts like a giant blanket that covers the whole planet. Heat gets trapped inside. Scientists call this the **greenhouse effect**.

Think! Think about the way your coat keeps you warm on cold days. What would happen if you wore your coat on a hot, sunny day? Venus' atmosphere is like a coat. Now you see why it gets so hot there!

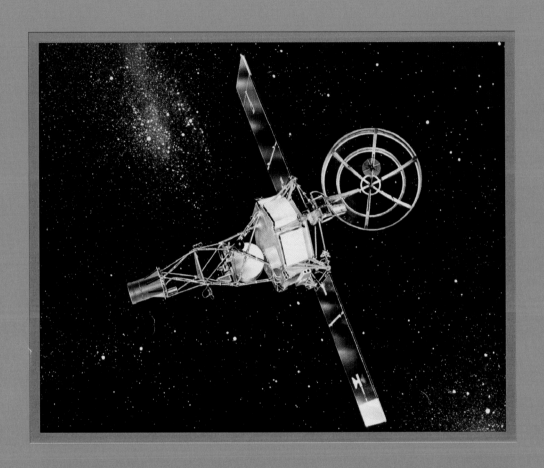

Mariner 2 was launched on August 27, 1962.

Scientists know a lot about Venus. They sent a spacecraft called *Mariner 2* to Venus in 1962. More than 20 other spacecraft have been to Venus since then.

There will always be new things to learn about Venus. What will we find out next?

GLOSSARY

atmosphere (AT-muhss-fihr) the gases or air surrounding a planet

axis (AK-siss) an imaginary line that goes through an object and around which the object turns

gravity (GRAV-uh-tee) the invisible force between objects in space that makes them pull on each other

greenhouse effect (GREEN-haus eff-EHKT) warming of a planet's surface caused when gases in the air trap heat

orbit (OR-bit) to travel in a path around a central point

Roman god (ROH-muhn GOD) one of many beings thought to have power over people and nature; the Romans were people who lived long ago in Rome or places ruled by Rome

rotate (ROH-tayt) spin

solar system (SOH-lur SISS-tuhm) a star, such as the Sun, and all the planets and moons that move around it

FIND OUT MORE

BOOKS

Aguilar, David A. *11 Planets: A New View of the Solar System*. Washington, DC: National Geographic Society, 2008.

Fleisher, Paul. *Venus*. Minneapolis: Lerner Publications, 2010.

Landau, Elaine. *Venus*. New York: Children's Press, 2008.

WEB SITES

HubbleSite Gallery
hubblesite.org/gallery
Take a look at some cool pictures of outer space.

NASA: Solar System Exploration
solarsystem.nasa.gov/kids
Check out these fun activities from NASA.

Space.com—Our Solar System: Facts, Formation and Discovery
www.space.com/solarsystem/
Learn more about the objects in our solar system and how they were formed.

INDEX

ABOUT THE AUTHOR

Ariel Kazunas lives on the Oregon coast, writing books for kids and working at the Sitka Center for Art and Ecology. She has also worked for several nonprofit magazines. Ariel loves exploring our planet, Earth—especially by hand, foot, bike, and boat—and camping out under the stars.